HAL•LEONARD
INSTRUMENTAL
PLAY-ALONG

CLARINET

twilight

HOW TO USE THE CD ACCOMPANIMENT:

THE CD IS PLAYABLE ON ANY CD PLAYER. FOR PC AND MAC USERS, THE CD IS ENHANCED
SO YOU CAN ADJUST THE RECORDING TO ANY TEMPO WITHOUT CHANGING PITCH.

A MELODY CUE APPEARS ON THE RIGHT CHANNEL ONLY. IF YOUR CD PLAYER HAS A BALANCE ADJUSTMENT,
YOU CAN ADJUST THE VOLUME OF THE MELODY BY TURNING DOWN THE RIGHT CHANNEL.

ISBN 978-1-4234-7459-3

HAL•LEONARD®
CORPORATION

7777 W. BLUEMOUND RD. P.O. BOX 13819 MILWAUKEE, WI 53213

Visit Hal Leonard Online at
www.halleonard.com

CONTENTS

◆ BELLA'S LULLABY

CLARINET

Composed by CARTER BURWELL

◆2 DECODE

CLARINET

Words and Music by TAYLOR YORK,
HAYLEY WILLIAMS and JOSH FARRO

❸ EYES ON FIRE

CLARINET

Words and Music by TOBIAS WILNER BERTRAM (KODA)
and KIRSTINE STUBBE TEGLBAERG (KODA)

◆ FULL MOON

CLARINET

Words and Music by THEO KEATING
and SIMON LORD

◆ 5 GO ALL THE WAY

(Into the Twilight)

Clarinet

Words and Music by ATTICUS ROSS, PERRY FARRELL,
ETTY LAU FARRELL and CARL RESTIVO

◆ LEAVE OUT ALL THE REST

Clarinet

Words and Music by MIKE SHINODA, JOE HAHN,
BRAD DELSON, ROB BOURDON,
CHESTER BENNINGTON and DAVE FARRELL

7 SPOTLIGHT
(Twilight Remix)

CLARINET

Words and Music by
PAUL MEANY

◆ SUPERMASSIVE BLACK HOLE

CLARINET

Words and Music by
MATTHEW BELLAMY

◆❾ TREMBLE FOR MY BELOVED

CLARINET

Words and Music by
ED ROLAND